TELE-*VIS*

Words to the Wise from TV's Greatest Characters

A Bruce Nash and Allan Zullo Book
Compiled by Sophie Nash

Andrews and McMeel
A Universal Press Syndicate Company
Kansas City

ISBN: 0-8362-0561-8

Designed by Barrie Maguire
Photos courtesy of Movie Star News, Eddie Brandt's Saturday Matinee, Cinema Collectors, and Larry Edmunds Bookshop, Inc.

Attention: Schools and Businesses:
Andrews and McMeel books are available at quantity discounts with bulk purchase for educational, business, or sales promotional use. For information, please write to Special Sales Department, Andrews and McMeel, 4900 Main Street, Kansas City, Missouri 64112.

DEDICATION   To all the talented television writers who
created the memorable characters whose
words of wisdom helped shape *our* character.

ACKNOWLEDGMENTS   A special thanks to Mike Fleiss, for helping to
get it all started.

Additional kudos to Robyn Nash, whose
knowledge of television knows no bounds.

TV LOOKS AT LIFE

Plato . . . Aristotle . . . Sartre . . . Nietzsche . . . these men have been called history's greatest philosophers. But now, a few new names have been added to the list: Kramden . . . Brady . . . Partridge . . . Bunker . . . Bundy . . . Munster.

Tele-Visions presents the philosophical musings of TV's most memorable characters. In this prime-time guide to better living, these televisionary thinkers tackle some of life's most important issues:

- Ed Norton on commitment: "As we say in the sewer, if you're not prepared to go all the way, don't put your boots on in the first place."

- Murphy Brown on discrimination: "I'd like to think that one day people won't be judged by their gender or the color of their skin, but by the things that really matter . . . like their taste in music. Motown."

- Jed Clampett on the good life: "Once you've tasted turkey you ain't likely to settle for tripe."

- Roseanne Conner on marriage: "Marriage is a life sentence with no chance for parole."

- Al Bundy on men: "Real men love girls, but hate women."

- Morticia Addams on patience: "A watched cauldron never boils."

- Archie Bunker on prayer: "You can sometimes pray too long to God . . . after that it ain't prayin', it's naggin'."

- Mr. Ed on sacrifice: "Some must suffer so that others may walk with their tails held high."

- Rob Petrie on success: "Behind every successful man, there's a woman with a big mouth."

Finally, here's a philosophical manifesto for that rare breed of intellectual known as the couch potato. Why bother espousing the philosophy of a Heidegger or Hegel when you can more easily quote Conner or Cartwright?

Tele-Visions brings out the philosopher in all of us. The revealing quotations in this book will make you think, wonder, and laugh. Best of all, you don't need a B.A., M.A., or Ph.D. to read it.

All you need is a love of television.

"It's just hard not to listen to TV—
it's spent so much more time raising us
than you have."

—**BART SIMPSON,** *"The Simpsons,"*
to his father, Homer

ACCURACY "Next time you want to pin somebody's hide to the barn, you'd better use facts for nails."
—**LOU GRANT,** *"Lou Grant"*

ACHIEVEMENT "When a donkey flies, you don't blame him for not staying up that long."
—**MURRAY SLAUGHTER,**
"The Mary Tyler Moore Show"

ADAPTING "That's the way life is. Sometimes they give you the wrong box and you have to be a good sport about it."
—**WOOD NEWTON,** *"Evening Shade"*

ADAPTING

"A little emotional flexibility is a good thing. It is the mighty oak that snaps and falls during a windstorm, but the weeping willow that's able to bend and see another day."
—**DR. FRASIER CRANE,** *"Frasier"*

ADAPTING   "Ladies and gentlemen, take my advice: Pull down your pants and slide on the ice."
—**DR. SIDNEY FREEDMAN,** *"M*A*S*H"*

ADULTHOOD   "I've been a kid, and I've been an adult. And believe me, adultery isn't what it's cracked up to be."
—**DANNY PARTRIDGE,** *"The Partridge Family"*

ADVERSITY   "When the tides of life turn against you
And the current upsets your boat,
Don't waste those tears on what might have been;
Just lay on your back and float."
—**ED NORTON,** *"The Honeymooners"*

AGING   "They say you're getting old when you stoop to tie your shoes and wonder what else you can do while you're down there."

—**SENATOR STROBE SMITHERS,** *"Hearts Afire"*

"And then one day you turn on the football game and the quarterback looks like your grandson."

—**LOU GRANT,** *"Lou Grant"*

"Honey, at my age, style is just getting all your buttons in the right holes."

—**BERNICE CLIFTON,** *"Designing Women"*

AGING "That's the great thing about senility. You're always meeting new people."
　　　　　　　—**FRAN FINE,** *"The Nanny"*

"After eighty, every year without a headstone is a milestone."
　　　　　　　—**SOPHIA PETRILLO,** *"The Golden Girls"*

ANARCHY "Where there is no law, there is no bread."
　　　　　　　—**PALADIN,** *"Have Gun Will Travel"*

ANTAGONISM "A man carries a chip on his shoulder too long, he acquires a permanent callus."
—**DR. BEN CASEY,** *"Ben Casey"*

APOLOGIZING "A fellow just hates to admit he's wrong. It takes a little courage to do it, and swallowing of pride, but it's one of the paths to wisdom."
—**JIM ANDERSON,** *"Father Knows Best"*

ASSERTIVENESS "Just 'cause I said 'yes' when we got married don't mean I gotta keep sayin' 'yes' the rest of my life."
—**EDITH BUNKER,** *"All in the Family"*

APPEARANCE

"Fashion tip: You don't want that tool belt to hang too low so it shows that unsightly butt crack."
—**TIM TAYLOR,**
"Home Improvement"

AVOIDING PROBLEMS

"Nip it! Nip it in the bud!"

—**BARNEY FIFE,** *"The Andy Griffith Show"*

BAD INFLUENCES

"If you lie down with dogs, you get up with fleas."

—**AMOS BURKE,** *"Burke's Law"*

BAD MANNERS

"Must genius and bad manners inevitably go hand-in-hand? If that's an immutable law of human nature, then I'm content to be a slob."

—**DR. TED HOFFMAN,** *"Ben Casey"*

BAD TIMING

"Always the way, isn't it? You're at your desk all morning doin' your job but the one minute you take to goof off is when the boss walks in."

—**OFFICER CARL LEVITT,** *"Barney Miller"*

THE BATTLE OF THE SEXES

"It's not prejudice. It's just that men are naturally superior drivers."
—**GREG BRADY,**
"The Brady Bunch"

BEAUTY   "Pa always says a homely polliwog makes a purty frog."
—**HOSS CARTWRIGHT,** *"Bonanza"*

"Beauty of the mind is more exciting than beauty of the flesh."
—**JANE HATHAWAY,** *"The Beverly Hillbillies"*

BEDSIDE   "Medicine is a lot more than credits and debits."
MANNERS   —**DR. DONALD WESTPHALL,** *"St. Elsewhere"*

BEGINNINGS "The journey of a thousand miles begins with a single step."
—**ANTHONY RUSSO,** *"Blossom"*

BEING PREPARED "If opportunity does knock, I want to know how much to be wearing when I answer the door."
—**JOE HACKETT,** *"Wings"*

BEING YOURSELF "Try accepting yourself as you are. . . . Then maybe everyone else can."
—**PETE DIXON,** *"Room 222"*

BETRAYAL "If you're gonna stab somebody in the back, the least you can do is look her in the eye."

—**COL. SHERMAN POTTER,** *"M*A*S*H"*

THE BLUES "There are only three cures for the blues: eating candy, doing your hair, and men."

—**LAURETTE BARBER,** *"China Beach"*

BREEDING "In leather goods, as in people, breeding is everything."

—**MAJ. CHARLES EMERSON WINCHESTER,** *"M*A*S*H"*

THE CHANGE OF LIFE

"Men have menopause too.
They just haven't had all the
bad press we women have."
—**MAUDE FINDLAY,**
"Maude"

CAUTION "Let's be careful out there."
>   —**SGT. PHIL ESTERHAUS,** *"Hill Street Blues"*

CHARISMA "Some people have [something]—it's kind of like a perfume—that makes everyone want to be around them."
>   —**DR. MICHAELA "MIKE" QUINN,**
>   *"Dr. Quinn, Medicine Woman"*

CHILD REARING "The way a parent deals with play can send a kid the wrong messages. Believe me, I know. It's one of the reasons I've been in therapy for fifteen years."
>   —**FRANK FONTANA,** *"Murphy Brown"*

CHILD REARING "Why can't children be more like a musical? Produce them, teach them a few catchy tunes, and send them on the road until they work out the kinks."
—**MAXWELL SHEFFIELD,** "*The Nanny*"

CHOICES "Sometimes you don't realize you've made the right choice until you get a chance to see the wrong one."
—**MADDIE HAYES,** *"Moonlighting"*

COMMITMENT "As we say in the sewer, if you're not prepared to go all the way, don't put your boots on in the first place."
—**ED NORTON,** *"The Honeymooners"*

COMMITMENT   "There comes a time in a man's life when he has to take the plunge or forever stand on the sidelines."
—**STEVEN KEATON,** *"Family Ties"*

"Life's a lot easier if you can avoid ever putting yourself on the line."
—**DANA PALLADINO,** *"Love and War"*

COMMON SENSE   "Ain't never yet seen a fish with sense enough to turn around and swim out the way he came."
—**HOSS CARTWRIGHT,** *"Bonanza"*

COMMUNICATION

"Big things . . . you talk over with your wife before you do what you woulda done anyway."
—**ARCHIE BUNKER,**
"All in the Family"

COMMUNICATION   "Language is the key to world peace."
—**BATMAN,** *"Batman"*

"That's what's so great about centerfolds. They don't talk back."
—**ALISON PARKER,** *"Melrose Place"*

COMMUNISM   "Why would you work at all if you know you're going to get an equal share?"
—**QUENTIN KELLY,** *"Grace Under Fire"*

COMPATIBILITY "If two people can dance well together, the chances are good they can make it."
—**JACK STEIN,** *"Love and War"*

COMPUTERS "Personally, I try to avoid machines that talk back."
—**BEN MATLOCK,** *"Matlock"*

CONSEQUENCES "You chose to live, now live with your choices."
—**JOYCE DAVENPORT,** *"Hill Street Blues"*

CONSERVATIVES "You conservatives are all alike—squeaky clean on the outside, but scratch the surface and nine times out of ten you'll find just another sophomoric fraternity boy in various stages of sexually arrested development."
—**GEORGIE ANNE LAHTI,** *"Hearts Afire"*

CONTROL "Give him an inch, he thinks he's a ruler."
—**DET. GINA NAVARRO CALABRESE,**
"Miami Vice"

COPING "Some people won't accept pain. They just refuse delivery."
—**DR. SIDNEY FREEDMAN,** *"M*A*S*H"*

COPS

"There's only two kinds of cop—
the quick and the dead!"
—**BARNEY FIFE,**
"The Andy Griffith Show"

CORRUPTION "Any large organization of powerful people, even if it's not conspiratorial, is open to excess and abuse."
—**DET. ARTHUR DIETRICH,**
"Barney Miller"

COURAGE "There's always a chance for a man who finds his courage."
—**BEN CARTWRIGHT,** *"Bonanza"*

CUTTING YOUR LOSSES "Better quit while you're behind."
—**CAPT. TRAPPER JOHN McINTYRE,**
*"M*A*S*H"*

DATING   "I'd give up on women. If only your kind didn't look so damn good naked."
                          —**JACK STEIN,** *"Love and War"*

"The only difference between a date and a job interview is not many job interviews is there a chance you'll end up naked at the end of it."
                          —**JERRY SEINFELD,** *"Seinfeld"*

"Why don't you forget about 'techniques' and stop trying so hard. If you didn't come on like a used car salesman, maybe girls would stop kicking you in the tires."
                          —**BOB HARTLEY,** *"The Bob Newhart Show"*

DATING

"A kite is like a really cute guy. You give him some slack and let him fly free, then, at the end of the day, you yank his string and reel him back in."
—FRAN FINE,
"The Nanny"

DATING "You don't tell boys to call you—you get them to call you by being mature—by playing it cool."
　　　　　　—**MARCIA BRADY,** *"The Brady Bunch"*

"Women like it when you ask them questions about themselves. Of course, then you have to listen to all their crap, but, hey, it's the price of admission."
　　　　　　—**KIP ZAKARIS,** *"Love and War"*

DEATH "Showing respect for the dead is important because the dead have an image problem."
　　　　　　—**ALEX P. KEATON,** *"Family Ties"*

DEATH   "Death ends a life but it doesn't end a relationship."
—**DR. DONALD WESTPHALL,** *"St. Elsewhere"*

"It's the people who are left who carry the scars."
—**DR. MICHAELA "MIKE" QUINN,**
"Dr. Quinn, Medicine Woman"

DEPENDABILITY   "You don't always have to be better than everybody else—with a rifle or anything else—as long as you can do what has to be done when it counts. Just having people call you the best isn't important."
—**LUCAS McCAIN,** *"The Rifleman"*

DESTINY "Destiny is a dark, twisting road."

  —**TOD STILES,** *"Route 66"*

DIETING "America can't live on just Lean Cuisine. Our belly is too big."

  —**MAURICE MINNIFIELD,** *"Northern Exposure"*

DISCRIMINATION "I'd like to think that one day people won't be judged by their gender or the color of their skin, but by the things that really matter . . . like their taste in music. Motown."

  —**MURPHY BROWN,** *"Murphy Brown"*

DIFFERENCES

"People aren't as different as we think. We may have different beliefs, but we're all pretty much alike."
—**SHIRLEY PARTRIDGE,**
"The Partridge Family"

DIVORCE "Where I come from, we don't have exes, just husbands and corpses."
—**NURSE LAVERNE TODD,** *"Empty Nest"*

DREAMS "Dreams are for children. Grown-ups have goals."
—**FRANKIE REED,** *"Sisters"*

DRINKING "Alcohol lowers inhibitions, fogs reality, and dulls the senses. You see, for some people that's bad."
—**HERMAN BROOKS'S GENIUS PERSONALITY TO HIS ANIMAL PERSONALITY,**
"Herman's Head"

"Drunken driving and drinking don't mix."
—**CAPT. HAWKEYE PIERCE,** *"M*A*S*H"*

DRUGS "Take too many (diet pills) and PMS starts to look like a vacation."

—**KELLY TAYLOR,** *"Beverly Hills 90210"*

DRUNKS "They can be meaner 'n a yellow jacket inside long drawers."

—**CHESTER GOODE,** *"Gunsmoke"*

EARLY RISERS "Those unfortunates who feel good in the morning should have the courtesy not to impose it on anyone else."

—**SALLY ROGERS,** *"The Dick Van Dyke Show"*

EMOTIONAL SCARS   "It's the little battlefields like ponds, and bedrooms, and schoolyards that can often leave the worst scars."
—**DR. SIDNEY FREEDMAN,** *"M*A*S*H"*

EMOTIONS   "It's not healthy keeping everything inside you, letting it all build up like a pressure cooker. Once it explodes, you have a hell of a time scraping your guts off the walls and ceiling."
—**TEDDY REED,** *"Sisters"*

ENTERPRISE   "As my daddy used to say, where there's a way there's a will."
—**J. R. EWING,** *"Dallas"*

EQUALITY   "Before all that equality crapola, you was a sweet, frightened wife."
—**ARCHIE BUNKER,** *"All in the Family"*

"We're all immigrants. Some of us just happened to come to America sooner than others."
—**DR. MICHAELA "MIKE" QUINN,**
"Dr. Quinn, Medicine Woman"

ETHICS   "I never break the law, I just bend it a little bit."
—**MASTER SGT. ERNIE BILKO,**
"The Phil Silvers Show"

EXPECTATIONS

"Nothing is ever going to be as wonderful as our expectation of it."
—CAPT. BARNEY MILLER,
"Barney Miller"

THE EXISTENCE OF GOD
"On a straight, cost-efficiency basis, you can't prove it. There's no annual report, no pictures of the board of directors."

—**ALEX P. KEATON,** *"Family Ties"*

EXPERIENCE
"You cannot teach that which you do not know."

—**JILL TAYLOR,** *"Home Improvement"*

FAIR PLAY
"You wanna rewrite the game plan, I'll rewrite the rules!"

—**DET. SONNY CROCKETT,** *"Miami Vice"*

FAKING IT
"Lookin' happy ain't bein' happy. Some mornin's I put on my happiness like it was makeup."

—**EDITH BUNKER,** *"All in the Family"*

FAME "If you stick your head above the crowd, sooner or later you're going to get hit by lightning."
—**MURPHY BROWN,** *"Murphy Brown"*

FATE "There aren't any accidents. Everything happens the way it's supposed to happen."
—**MALLORY KEATON,** *"Family Ties"*

"You're sort of like an arrow, you know? You're aiming at your mark, but . . . the wind gets you."
—**CARLY WATKINS,** *"The John Larroquette Show"*

FATE   "Everything in life comes and goes. The things that matter to us most are taken from us just when we can least afford to lose them. And in the end, all the things we strive for come to nothing."
—**DIANE CHAMBERS,** *"Cheers"*

"Even though things may not happen like we planned, they can work out anyway."
—**ROZ DOYLE,** *"Frasier"*

FEAR   "Without fear one would stand in traffic and get run over. It's nature's way of protecting your life."
—**FATHER FRANCIS MULCAHY,** *"M*A*S*H"*

FEAR   "Anybody looks big to a scared kid."
>> —**COMMISSIONER TONY SCALI,**
> *"The Commish"*

"The fear of death is the shadow of the fear of life. To live in harmony with living things is to banish fear."
>> —**MASTER KAN,** *"Kung Fu"*

"All men have fears, but those who face their fears with dignity have courage as well."
>> —**ALEX RIEGER,** *"Taxi"*

FEAR "When you're scared of so many things . . . especially change . . . you end up falling back on all these safety nets."

—**JO REYNOLDS,** *"Melrose Place"*

FOOD "Food ain't supposed to be a luxury. . . . I mean, it's supposed to keep you alive, it ain't supposed to provide entertainment value."

—**ROSEANNE CONNER,** *"Roseanne"*

FREE SPEECH "I don't agree with what you've just said but I will defend to my death your right to say it."

—**CAPT. B.J. HUNNICUT,** *"M*A*S*H"*

FEELINGS

"An insult to a man with no feelings is like hay fever to a man with no nose."
—MORK,
"Mork and Mindy"

FREE SPEECH "Free speech is great, until it's someone else speaking."
—**REUBEN KINCAID,** *"The Partridge Family"*

FRIENDSHIP "When you start putting a price on friendship, you find out your friendship isn't worth a nickel."
—**BOB HARTLEY,** *"The Bob Newhart Show"*

FUNNY PEOPLE "All funny people have a certain amount of . . . rage . . . bubbling beneath the surface."
—**JEANNIE SANDERS,** *"The Larry Sanders Show"*

GAMBLING

"A sucker's groan is music
to a gambler's ear."
—**MASTER SGT. ERNIE BILKO,**
"The Phil Silvers Show"

GENEROSITY "He who is openhearted is kingly."
—**KWAI CHANG CAINE,** *"Kung Fu"*

GETTING THE POINT "You don't have to have the tree fall on you to know that it made a sound."
—**TOBY PEDALBEE,** *"Dream On"*

THE GOOD LIFE "Once you've tasted turkey you ain't likely to settle for tripe."
—**JED CLAMPETT,** *"The Beverly Hillbillies"*

GROWING UP "It was a lot easier being a girl than it is being a woman."
—**ALEX HALSEY,** *"Sisters"*

GROWING UP "Just because a bird leaves the nest doesn't mean it's going to be creamed by the Concorde."
—**DAN CONNER,** *"Roseanne"*

"You grow up thinking that your dad knows so much more than you, then . . . you realize he wasn't any smarter, he was just taller."
—**ANTHONY RUSSO,** *"Blossom"*

"But as with all transitional objects, be they a teddy bear, be they a thumb, be they a blanket, be they a chair . . . there comes a time when the healthy thing is to put these security objects aside and reassert your independence."
—**NILES CRANE,** *"Frasier"*

GROWING UP "If you hate high school, wait'll you get a load of life."
—**NICK RUSSO,** *"Blossom"*

HEAD OF THE HOUSE "The wearer of the pants don't take orders from the wearer of the bloomers."
—**ARCHIE BUNKER,** *"All in the Family"*

HELPING A FRIEND "The question isn't: Why? The question is: What?"
—**TOD STILES,** *"Route 66"*

HAVING CHILDREN

"Some parents get better children than they deserve."
—PERRY MASON,
"Perry Mason"

HONESTY   "It takes a really honest person to admit they're a liar."
—**JOEY GLADSTONE,** *"Full House"*

"If you've got nothing to hide, you've nothing to fret over."
—**JESSICA FLETCHER,** *"Murder, She Wrote"*

"To suppress a truth is to give it force beyond endurance."
—**MASTER KAN,** *"Kung Fu"*

HONESTY "What's so great about this honesty thing? You'd think it was some sort of religion or something."
—**COACH HAYDEN FOX,** *"Coach"*

HUSBANDS "You are the king because a man's home is his castle, and in that castle, you're the king."
—**RALPH KRAMDEN,** *"The Honeymooners"*

IDEALISM "In our jet-propelled society, idealism dies a lingering death."
—**DR. DAVID ZORBA,** *"Ben Casey"*

IDEALISM "Anyone can make money. Only a few can make a difference."

 —**AMOS BURKE,** *"Burke's Law"*

IMAGE "I think this human being image is gonna get me more action than cheap wine."

 —**SAM MALONE,** *"Cheers"*

INDEPENDENCE "If you want to keep your feet on the ground—pull yourself up by your own bootstraps."

 —**MAJ. FRANK BURNS,** *"M*A*S*H"*

THE IMPORTANCE OF EDUCATION

"If you couldn't read,
you wouldn't be able to look
up what's on television, either."
—BEAVER CLEAVER,
"Leave It to Beaver"

INDIVIDUALITY   "Each of us must dance to his own tune."
    —**MAJ. CHARLES EMERSON WINCHESTER,**
    "M*A*S*H"

INFIDELITY   "Infidelity is as American as apple pie. Why . . . without infidelity there would be no 'Dynasty' . . . no 'Divorce Court' . . . no Ann Landers."
    —**DAVID ADDISON,** *"Moonlighting"*

INTERIOR DECORATING   "All I need is a comfortable place to park my fanny."
    —**MARTIN CRANE,** *"Frasier"*

JINXED　　"Bad luck follows the guilty."

—**PAUL BUCHMAN,** *"Mad About You"*

THE JOYS OF LIFE　"In one lifetime, a man knows many pleasures: A mother's smile in waking hours, a young woman's intimate searing touch, and the laughter of grandchildren in the twilight years. To deny these in ourselves is to deny that which makes us one with nature."

—**MASTER KAN,** *"Kung Fu"*

"Kicking ass in the morning is better than cappuccino."

—**ARTIE,** *"The Larry Sanders Show"*

THE JOYS OF LIFE   "Unless you're able to marvel at the wonder of a sunset, rejoice at seeing a baby stand up for the first time . . . and feel close on the inside to the people you're close to on the outside . . . unless you're able to do those things . . . aren't you already in prison?"
—**MORK**, *"Mork and Mindy"*

JUDGMENT DAY   "When you try to add up what a man's life means, you don't just count the things against him. . . . You can't just cross out all the years of bein' decent and doin' a job—for one dark night when he runs off with somebody else's money."
—**THE VIRGINIAN**, *"The Virginian"*

JUDGMENT DAY "If there's justice in the universe, the deity has reserved a special circle in Hell for the Repo Man."
—**SGT. PHIL ESTERHAUS,** *"Hill Street Blues"*

JUDGING CHARACTER "It's what's under the hood that counts, my man."
—**BRANDON WALSH,** *"Beverly Hills 90210"*

JUSTICE "It's never too late for justice."
—**SHIRLEY PARTRIDGE,** *"The Partridge Family"*

KINDNESS "People should treat people good when they're alive instead of tryin' to make up for it after they're dead."
—**DET. MICK BELKER,** *"Hill Street Blues"*

KISSING UP "If we're going to kiss some ass can it at least be in a tight skirt?"
—**HERMAN'S ANIMAL PERSONALITY,** *"Herman's Head"*

LIFE "Expect the worst and hope for the best."
—**BRENDA WALSH,** *"Beverly Hills 90210"*

"Life is not all lovely thorns and singing vultures, you know."

—MORTICIA ADDAMS,
"The Addams Family"

LIFE AND DEATH "Before new people can get on the ride, some of the folks who've been riding it for a while, they have to get off."

— **DAVE BARRY,** *"Dave's World"*

LIMITATIONS "You only go around once in this life and there's just not enough gusto for everybody."

— **OFFICER CARL LEVITT,** *"Barney Miller"*

LOSERS "I have one very firm rule in my life—I don't eat at the same table, bet on the same side, or climb on the same airplane with losers."

— **LOUIE DE PALMA,** *"Taxi"*

LOSERS "You know, you shouldn't put down a loser . . . because you might be one yourself one day."
—**CAROL BRADY,** *"The Brady Bunch"*

LOSING YOUR TEMPER "You know what they say: You catch more flies with honey than you do going berserk."
—**ASSISTANT COACH LUTHER VAN DAM,** *"Coach"*

LOVE "One of the troubles with love—makes you soft, makes you take the easy way out for somebody."
—**BUZ MURDOCK,** *"Route 66"*

LOVE "You don't hold a man's head out of the toilet for five years unless there's some real feeling there."
—**JOHN HEMINGWAY,**
"The John Larroquette Show"

"When you love somebody, you're always in trouble. There's only two things you can do about it: Either stop loving 'em or love 'em a whole lot more."
—**COL. SHERMAN POTTER,** *"M*A*S*H"*

"In this day and age, anything can happen. Love does not ask to see your I.D."
—**KEITH PARTRIDGE,** *"The Partridge Family"*

LOVE

"Well, you know what they say,
lucky in love, unlucky with fruit."
—JERRY SEINFELD,
"Seinfeld"

LOVE "It's not love. He's just my boyfriend, that's all."
                                   —**KATHY "KITTEN" ANDERSON,**
                                   "Father Knows Best"

LOVE AFFAIRS "You know the romance is gone when passion gives way to good manners."
                                   —**ANN KELSEY,** *"L.A. Law"*

LUCK "Lightning strikes one in a million and you think, it'll never happen to me, but you hear one in a million could hit the lottery and you figure, hey, somebody's got to win."
                                   —**DAVE BARRY,** *"Dave's World"*

LUCK   "I suppose that's the way it goes in the Manhunt Game
. . . sometimes you bag 'em, sometimes you don't."
—**ANDY TAYLOR,** *"The Andy Griffith Show"*

MACHISMO   "I thought we'd advanced beyond the notion that a
real man is one who risks his life in pointless flirtations
with death."
—**DR. FRASIER CRANE,** *"Cheers"*

"If a man feels pain from anything less than a gunshot
wound, he's weak."
—**JACK STEIN,** *"Love and War"*

MAKING LOVE "And the Ruba says, you should avoid making love where cattle have walked in the past three days."
—**LOUISE FITZER,** *"Herman's Head"*

"Sweat is an underrated but very effective aphrodisiac."
—**MAURICE MINNIFIELD,** *"Northern Exposure"*

MANKIND "I got nothin' against mankind. It's people I don't trust."
—**ARCHIE BUNKER,** *"All in the Family"*

MARITAL ADVICE "Don't point out the fact that the hair he's losing on his head is now growing out of his nose . . . and ears."
—**PEG BUNDY,** *"Married . . . with Children"*

MARRIAGE "Marriage is a life sentence with no chance for parole."
—**ROSEANNE CONNER,** *"Roseanne"*

"The important thing is to marry a man who loves you, because if he loves you, you can get away with murder."
—**LISA DOUGLAS,** *"Green Acres"*

MARRIAGE   "Well it is sort of like a trap, isn't it? It looks really good from a distance, you go into it with the best intentions, and a year later you're willing to chew your own leg off to get out of it."
—**SIX WILSON,** *"Blossom"*

"Fighting is what keeps a marriage together."
—**ROSEANNE CONNER,** *"Roseanne"*

"Every day you make choices . . . what side you're gonna part your hair on . . . caf or decaf . . . leaded or unleaded . . . whole wheat or rye . . . But you can change your mind. . . . You can't do that with a marriage. . . . You make your choice and it's rye toast every day."
—**DAVID ADDISON,** *"Moonlighting"*

MARRIAGE

"You women always know
how to get revenge on us men.
You marry us."
—RALPH KRAMDEN,
"The Honeymooners"

MARRIAGE

"Marriage is like a birthday candle—the flames of passion burn brightest when the wick of intimacy is first ignited, but soon the heat of familiarity causes the wax of boredom to drip all over the vanilla frosting of novelty and the shredded coconut of romance."
—**DAVE BARRY,** *"Dave's World"*

"I happen to believe in the sanctity of marriage—no matter how ugly or disgusting it gets."
—**MAJ. FRANK BURNS,** *"M*A*S*H"*

"Marriage is like an onion. Each divorce is like peeling another layer of the onion. There's a lot of tears, but you gotta keep peeling until you get to the good part."
—**NADINE SWOBODA,** *"Grace Under Fire"*

MARRIAGE "Just like this sander vibrates in harmony with the wood, we men have to learn to vibrate in harmony with our wives."

—**TIM TAYLOR,** *"Home Improvement"*

"If this is marriage, I'm dying a bachelor."

—**BILLY CAMPBELL,** *"Melrose Place"*

MATURITY "I guess it takes a certain amount of maturity to admit you acted like an idiot."

—**COACH HAYDEN FOX,** *"Coach"*

MEDDLING

"If you don't see the difference between honest concern and meddling, then you're ignorant or insensitive or both."
—**OLIVIA WALTON,**
"The Waltons"

MEMORIES "Strange thing about memories . . . they can be more real than anything we call reality."
—**ALEX P. KEATON,** *"Family Ties"*

MEN "Hey, did it ever occur to you that men are not incapable of change . . . that maybe we just don't want to?"
—**COACH HAYDEN FOX,** *"Coach"*

"Men can't be rushed, they're like chicken. You cook them too fast they get tough . . . you take your time, let them simmer a while, they fall apart in your hands."
—**FRAN FINE,** *"The Nanny"*

MEN   "With men, if you ask for something, you'll never get it. But if you do some damage to their internal organs, you've got a shot."
—**PEG BUNDY,** *"Married . . . with Children"*

"A man's head is like a doorknob . . . any woman can turn it."
—**BUB O'CASEY,** *"My Three Sons"*

"Believe me, if they sold men at Labels For Less, I'd have one on layaway."
—**FRAN FINE,** *"The Nanny"*

MEN

"Men have no judgment
when it comes to women."
—**NORM PETERSON,**
"Cheers"

MEN　"If men enjoy eating and drinking at home, they never take you anywhere."
　　　　　　　　　　　　　—**PEG BUNDY,** *"Married . . . with Children"*

"If there was no sports and no women the only thing guys would ever say is, 'So what's in the refrigerator?'"
　　　　　　　　　　　　　—**JERRY SEINFELD,** *"Seinfeld"*

"Real men love girls, but hate women."
　　　　　　　　　　　　　—**AL BUNDY,** *"Married . . . with Children"*

MENSTRUATION   "Then when it finally stops, you go through meno-pause, lose your mind for a while, grow facial hair, and start sounding like Darth Vader."
  —**SIX WILSON,** *"Blossom"*

MONEY   "There's only one thing more valuable than money—more money."
  —**DANNY PARTRIDGE,** *"The Partridge Family"*

"Money is something you never spend . . . you just make more of it."
  —**THURSTON HOWELL III,** *"Gilligan's Island"*

MOOD SWINGS "My biggest fear is that there is no such thing as PMS, and this is who I really am."
—**CAROL WESTON,** *"Empty Nest"*

MORTALITY "I suppose we'd all give up today for one more tomorrow. Yet no sentence is complete without a period."
—**DR. DAVID ZORBA,** *"Ben Casey"*

MOTHERS "A mother never stops feeling responsible."
—**OLIVIA WALTON,** *"The Waltons"*

NATURE "All creatures, the low and the high, are one with nature. If we have the wisdom to learn, all may teach us their virtues."

— **MASTER KAN,** *"Kung Fu"*

NEATNESS "A pile for everything and everything in its pile."

— **COL. SHERMAN POTTER,** *"M*A*S*H"*

NEWS "News is truth."

— **LOU GRANT,** *"The Mary Tyler Moore Show"*

NEW YEAR'S RESOLUTIONS "Like most people, I made the damn things every New Year, and by the opening of spring training they were a forgotten memory, like last season's point spread."
—**MOLLY DODD,**
"The Days and Nights of Molly Dodd"

NICE GUYS "Nice guys always make me suspicious."
—**COMMISSIONER TONY SCALI,**
"The Commish"

PACIFICISM "I'll treat their wounds, heal their wounds, bind their wounds, but I will not inflict their wounds."
—**CAPT. HAWKEYE PIERCE,** *"M*A*S*H"*

PACIFICISM "If there is no contention, there is neither defeat nor victory. The supple willow does not contend against the storm, yet it survives."
— **MASTER KAN,** *"Kung Fu"*

PACING YOURSELF "Life is like a red Ford . . . and you're better off putting that Ford in neutral than revving your engine all the time."
— **JIM ROCKFORD,** *"The Rockford Files"*

PAIN "Through pain comes growth."
— **GRACE SHEFFIELD,** *"The Nanny"*

PARANOIA   "You know, there's one good thing about being paranoid. You're always the center of attention."
       —**LAURIE PARTRIDGE,** *"The Partridge Family"*

PATIENCE   "A watched cauldron never boils."
       —**MORTICIA ADDAMS,** *"The Addams Family"*

"Sometimes you just got to chill out and let it happen."
       —**BRANDON WALSH,** *"Beverly Hills 90210"*

PATIENCE

"Spooks a man—knowin' there's
nothin' he can do but wait."
—HOSS CARTWRIGHT,
"Bonanza"

PATIENCE   "Sometimes the best thing you can do is nothing."
                —**WILSON**, *"Home Improvement"*

PEER PRESSURE   "It doesn't matter what people think about what you
                do. What counts is that you feel right about it."
                —**JIM ROCKFORD**, *"The Rockford Files"*

PERSEVERANCE   "There's no place in America for quitters."
                —**J.D. PICKETT**, *"The Waltons"*

PICKING UP GIRLS   "I usually figure something good has happened if the girl hasn't given me a phony name."
         —**JERRY ROBINSON,** *"The Bob Newhart Show"*

PITY   "I've gotten many things in my life out of pity. It doesn't make them any less pleasurable."
         —**BRIAN HACKETT,** *"Wings"*

POTENTIAL   "To watch a talent grow is to cultivate an angry impatience—knowing what such a man could become, were it not for life's frustrating brevity."
         —**DR. DAVID ZORBA,** *"Ben Casey"*

POWER "Nobody can give you power. Real power is something you take."

—**JOCK EWING,** *"Dallas"*

PRAYER "You can sometimes pray too long to God . . . after that it ain't prayin', it's naggin'."

—**ARCHIE BUNKER,** *"All in the Family"*

PRIDE IN ONE'S WORK "There are many inspiring sights in this world . . . the *Mona Lisa,* Michelangelo's *David,* the Parthenon. . . . But to me, nothing can equal the beauty of a delicately wrought piece of surgery."

—**DR. DAVID ZORBA,** *"Ben Casey"*

PRIORITIES

"Never put the hearse
before the horse."
—**GRANDPA MUNSTER,**
"The Munsters"

PRIORITIES   "You can't do every silly thing you want to in life. You have to make your choices and you have to try to be happy with them."
                   —**JACK ARNOLD,** *"The Wonder Years"*

PROCRASTINATION   "Like we say in the sewer, time and tide wait for no man."
                        —**ED NORTON,** *"The Honeymooners"*

"Why put off what you can do today?"
—**DET. SONNY CROCKETT,**
"Miami Vice"

PROTESTING "There is something I can do. I can raise my voice to say the most important word there is—no!"
—**TEDDY REED,** *"Sisters"*

PRUDENCE "Do your celebratin', but stay out of trouble."
—**MARSHAL MATT DILLON,** *"Gunsmoke"*

REALITY "Real life is not a Nike commercial."
—**RHONDA BLAIR,** *"Melrose Place"*

REBELLION   "I was kind of a rebel munchkin, if you will. . . . In fact, in my coloring book, I used to color outside the lines . . . on purpose."

—**JESSE KATSOPOLIS,** *"Full House"*

REEVALUATION   "If you can't find what you're looking for, you're looking for the wrong thing."

—**AMOS BURKE,** *"Burke's Law"*

REPRISAL   "Let's keep in mind that we only buy more trouble . . . when we wreak vengeance on the bearer of bad tidings."

—**SGT. PHIL ESTERHAUS,** *"Hill Street Blues"*

REPUTATION

"Steal my feedbag,
but not my good name."
—MR. ED,
"Mr. Ed"

RESPECT "When you respect somebody, it's not hard to stick up for him, no matter what his views are."
—**STEVEN KEATON,** *"Family Ties"*

RICH WOMEN "You show me a girl with enough money and I'll show you a raving beauty. I don't care what she looks like."
—**MILBURN DRYSDALE,** *"The Beverly Hillbillies"*

ROMANCE "To me the perfect dinner for two always includes a half-off coupon."
—**ROSEANNE CONNER,** *"Roseanne"*

ROMANCE   "Being sentimental can lead you to do things you regret later."

> —**MAJ. MARGARET "HOT LIPS" HOULIHAN,**
> *"M*A*S*H"*

RULES   "A rule is a rule and let's face it, without rules, there's chaos."

> —**COSMO KRAMER,** *"Seinfeld"*

SACRIFICE   "Some must suffer so that others may walk with their tails held high."

> —**MR. ED,** *"Mr. Ed"*

SACRIFICE

"At times one must deny their nature, sacrifice their own personal beliefs to protect another."
—LT. COMMANDER DATA,
"Star Trek: The Next Generation"

SANTA CLAUS "I believe in anyone who delivers."
—**FRAN FINE,** *"The Nanny"*

SCORING "I'm not the ladies' man everybody thinks I am. I bought a waterbed three years ago, and I'm still waiting to get seasick."
—**JERRY ROBINSON,** *"The Bob Newhart Show"*

SECURITY "You know, when you feel there's no one else in the world on your side, there's nothing like a kiss . . . to make you realize you don't need anybody else."
—**ROB PETRIE,** *"The Dick Van Dyke Show"*

SELF-REALIZATION "I think you should do what you want. In thirty years, nobody will ever remember you were alive anyway."
—**WOOD NEWTON,** *"Evening Shade"*

SERENITY "There's a time for battles and a time for peace— inner damn peace."
—**DR. DONALD WESTPHALL,** *"St. Elsewhere"*

"In strength is serenity."
—**MAJ. MARGARET "HOT LIPS" HOULIHAN,** *"M*A*S*H"*

SERENITY "Weakness prevails over strength, gentleness conquers. Become the calm and restful breeze that tames the violent sea."

—**MASTER KAN,** *"Kung Fu"*

SETTING LIMITS "There are two things I won't do for money—kill and get married."

—**JIM ROCKFORD,** *"The Rockford Files"*

"I can take umbrage, I can take the cake, I can take the A-train, I can take two and call me in the morning. But I cannot take this sitting down."

—**CAPT. HAWKEYE PIERCE,** *"M*A*S*H"*

SEX "You know, if you men had to have some of these babies, you'd be a lot more careful about where you park your Pontiacs."
—**FRIEDA EVANS,** *"Evening Shade"*

"Fifteen minutes of fun. A lifetime of regret."
—**KELLY TAYLOR,** *"Beverly Hills 90210"*

"You don't have to like her, Herm, this is sex we're talking about, not camping."
—**JAY NICHOLS,** *"Herman's Head"*

SHORTCUTS "You gotta cut corners or it could take two days to learn what you can get in two minutes."
　　　　　　—JIM ROCKFORD, *"The Rockford Files"*

SHOWERS "Hot showers for a cold. Cold showers for the hots."
　　　　　　—COL. SHERMAN POTTER, *"M*A*S*H"*

SHOWING AFFECTION "Remember what Mom always said: A handshake is as good as a hug."
　　　　　　—NILES CRANE, *"Frasier"*

SIN "The good die young, that they may not be corrupted; the wicked live on, that they may have a chance to repent."

—**PALADIN,** *"Have Gun Will Travel"*

SMOKING "Keep up the smoking, you guys: You'll stunt your growth, your liver will turn yellow, and your teeth'll all fall out onto your body and stab your toes."

—**CHET KINCAID,** *"The Bill Cosby Show"*

SOBRIETY "It's fun getting up without the wrath of grapes."

—**CAPT. HAWKEYE PIERCE,** *"M*A*S*H"*

SPONTANEITY "I like spontaneity as much as the next guy. I just need a little warning so it doesn't come completely out of nowhere."
—**JOE HACKETT,** *"Wings"*

STAYING YOUNG "Acting young isn't what keeps you young, but if you've got some memories, some good memories, of when you were young, that's what keeps you young."
—**RALPH KRAMDEN,** *"The Honeymooners"*

STUBBORNNESS "It's like, after you've been shot up by a lot of bullets and you're still alive—and you just have to keep looking for that last one that will finish you off—the one that gets you right between the eyes."
—**GEORGIE ANNE LAHTI,** *"Hearts Afire"*

STUPIDITY "Stupid is as stupid does."
  —**BEN MATLOCK,** *"Matlock"*

SUCCESS "Don't say 'but.' That little word 'but' is the difference between success and failure."
  —**MASTER SGT. ERNIE BILKO,**
  "The Phil Silvers Show"

"Hasn't it pretty much been accepted that a real man can be defined as one who makes gobs and gobs of money?"
  —**DR. FRASIER CRANE,** *"Cheers"*

"Behind every successful man, there's a woman with a big mouth."
  —**ROB PETRIE,** *"The Dick Van Dyke Show"*

SUCCESS

"Behind every successful business-man, you will find a woman. Just don't let that man's wife find her."
—**THURSTON HOWELL III,**
"Gilligan's Island"

SURVIVAL OF THE FITTEST "The old and weak get knocked off, the young and strong survive. It's the law of the jungle."
—**MAJ. FRANK BURNS,** *"M*A*S*H"*

TAKING RISKS "I'd rather die like a fool than live like a coward."
—**WOODY BOYD,** *"Cheers"*

TEACHERS "Teachers never die. They live in your memory forever."
—**KEVIN ARNOLD,** *"The Wonder Years"*

TELEVISION   "TV is always right."

  —**HOMER SIMPSON,** *"The Simpsons"*

"Television is nothing but a game of three-card monte designed to keep the natives distracted while the nation goes to hell."

  —**GENE KINSELLA,** *"Murphy Brown"*

"Violence on TV may be funny, but it's not so funny when that violence is happening to you."

  —**MARGE SIMPSON,** *"The Simpsons"*

TOUGH LOVE   "It's kind of liberating to find out you can scream at someone and still love them."

  —**STUART MARKOWITZ,** *"L. A. Law"*

TRUST   "Never trust a man who smells too good."
            —**LAURETTE BARBER,** *"China Beach"*

"You can always trust a man with a beer belly. . . . He don't have to steal so he can afford champagne."
            —**ARCHIE BUNKER,** *"All in the Family"*

TRUTHFULNESS   "Suspects may say what they want but the facts speak for themselves."
            —**PETER BURKE,** *"Burke's Law"*

TRUTHFULNESS

"The truth may be fine for philosophers and mathematicians . . . but when it comes to human relationships, one good lie and a little kindness is worth a thousand truths."

— **DAVID ADDISON,** *"Moonlighting"*

UNPLANNED PREGNANCY

"An accident is something you wouldn't do if you could do it all over again, but a surprise is something you didn't know you wanted until you had it."

— **ROSEANNE CONNER,** *"Roseanne"*

"If we're going to make a commitment the gravity of which will reverberate throughout our entire lives, we cannot do it in the throes of passion."

— **DR. FRASIER CRANE,** *"Frasier"*

VICES "Booze is the only thing that's bad for people that's still legal."

—**ARCHIE BUNKER,** *"All in the Family"*

VISIONARIES "It's the people who dream about what life should be that make the changes."

—**ORDERLY LUTHER HAWKINS,** *"St. Elsewhere"*

WAR "Every war has its 'ooms. You got doom, gloom, everybody ends up in a tomb, the planes zoom and bomb your room."

—**CAPT. HAWKEYE PIERCE,** *"M*A*S*H"*

WAR "You know what happens to good little soldiers—they go to the front and never come back."
—**TEDDY REED,** *"Sisters"*

WOMEN "The world started goin' to pot when they taught women to write."
—**ARCHIE BUNKER,** *"All in the Family"*

"Chicks are like buses—you miss one, another will come along before you know it."
—**ROY BIGGINS,** *"Wings"*

WOMEN "Women don't kill for money . . . they marry for it."
—**DAVID ADDISON**, *"Moonlighting"*

"When a woman says it's nothing, it's probably something, but if she says it's something, then forget it."
—**BUDDY SORRELL**, *"The Dick Van Dyke Show"*

WORKMANSHIP "Why are we bashing the Japanese? It's not their fault nobody's buying American. We can build a Patriot Missile, but we can't build a toaster oven that lasts more than a year."
—**JACK STEIN**, *"Love and War"*